# Where I Live

Written by Amy White

Hi! My name is Marcella.

This is where I live.

Where I live, there is a grocery store.
Sometimes, they give me an apple.

Where I live, there is a post office.

I like to write letters.

This is where I mail my letters.

Where I live, there is a park.

It has ball fields, trees, and grass.

The playground is what I like the best.

Where I live, there is a school.

I walk to school.

Some children come on the bus.

Where I live, there is a library.

The library has books you can take and read.

Then you bring the books back.

It is free!

Where I live, there is a gas station.
Some people get their cars fixed here.
Other people get their cars washed here.

Where I live, there is a pizza shop.
We get pizza once every two weeks.
It is a real treat!

Where I live, there is a bakery.
The fresh bread smells so good.

Where I live, there is a fire station.
The big red trucks have loud sirens!

Where I live, there is an office building.

A lot of people work here.

My doctor's office is here.

Where I live, there is a subway stop.
My mother rides the subway to work.

Can you guess where we are now?
This is my house.

What is it like where you live?